TAHA MUHAMMAD ALI

NEVER MIND

TWENTY POEMS AND A STORY

Translated by
Peter Cole, Yahya Hijazi, Gabriel Levin

IBIS

ACKNOWLEDGMENTS

Earlier versions of these poems were published in *PN Review, Parnassus in Review, Modern Poetry in Translation, The Jerusalem Post,* and *The Palestine-Israel Journal.* Grateful acknowledgment is due to the editors of these journals.

Author photo by Erwin Schenkelbach is courtesy of Mishkenot Sha'ananim.

ISBN 965-90125-2-7

IBIS EDITIONS
POB 8074
German Colony
Jerusalem
Israel

CONTENTS

Introduction   13

Abd El-Hadi Fights a Superpower   39
Post-Operative Complications Following
   the Extraction of Memory   41
Thrombosis in the Veins of Petroleum   43
Crack in the Skull   46
Warning   50
Fooling the Killers   51
Exodus   54
Ambergris   57
The Evening Wine of Aged Sorrow   61
Three Qasidas   67
Maybe   70
Empty Words   72
Twigs   75
The Height of Love   78

Sabha's Rope   81
Meeting at an Airport   85
Never Mind   88
This is the Collapsing Steel Mihrab, and
    That's My Mother, Before She Ceased to
    Mourn   91
Abd El-Hadi the Fool   93
The Kid Goats of Jamil   98

So What   103

INTRODUCTION

HAVING FOUND TAHA MUHAMMAD ALI'S store on Casanova Street in the old quarter of Nazareth empty, I sat on one of the small, wicker-topped stools and let my eyes roam about the shop. The shelves running up to the high, vaulted ceiling were crammed with imitation pearl-studded scabbards, ceramic bowls of various shapes and sizes, colorful kaffiyehs, olive-wood camels, inlaid boxes, nargilehs, postcards of the Crusader church rising above the shops at the end of the narrow street.

This wasn't exactly what I had expected. Some months earlier, when I'd first tried to translate two of Taha Muhammad Ali's poems, I had been told by a friend, who was then editing an anthology of Palestinian poetry, that the poet was a dealer in antiquities. Ali was born and raised, my friend had explained, in the village of Saffuriya, located on the site of what had once been the ancient town of Sepphoris, and at the age of seventeen was forced to leave with his family for Lebanon, after his village was razed to the ground by the Israeli army in the Arab–Israeli war of 1948. A year later he and his family slipped back across the border and eventually settled in Nazareth.

Ali, I now realized, was the proud owner of a souvenir shop. The only objects that might have passed for antiquities were some old farming implements and, leaning against the wall in one corner of the room, a waist-high jug, once used by villagers for storing grain.

*

A slim young man entered the shop and introduced himself as Nizar, the poet's son. Taha would soon arrive, he announced. For some time now he and his younger brother had run the store. Their father, Nizar added, would show up on occasion only to disappear into the nearby shops to sip Turkish coffee with his old friends. I wondered whether one of the shopkeepers wasn't the friend Ali had spoken of several weeks earlier in Jerusalem, at the city's Third International Poetry Festival. The poet had prefaced the reading of his poems by telling us, in halting Hebrew, "a little story."

Many years ago, he said, he had started up a small stand along the street leading into the Old City market in Nazareth where he would display small, lacquered camels made of olive wood and sell them to tourists who came from all parts of the world to visit the Church of the Annunciation. A certain friend of his used to visit him at the end of his workday and sit on the wooden stool he'd set out for him, so he could enjoy looking at the foreign passersby. "I would ask him to listen to a poem I had written the previous night," Ali told us,

> and he would refuse loudly: "I don't want to hear it! I'm tired and I want to rest." One day it occurred to me that I might "bribe" him, by offering him one of the small wooden camels in exchange for his listening to my new poem. When I stretched out my hand to offer him the camel, a not unmysterious smile came across his face, and he took the camel, put it in his pocket, and offered me—of his two

ears—only half an ear, with which he listened to my poem, all the while directing his eyes and his other ear-and-a-half to the people who were coming and going on the street before him, without there appearing on his face any indication that he was listening to me at all.

Time passed, and I continued to give my friend camels in exchange for his listening to each new poem that I wrote. On one of these afternoons, wanting to save myself a camel, I announced to my friend that Jean-Paul Sartre had visited Nazareth, and that the city council had invited me to participate in a reception for him where I met and spoke with him at length. My friend cut me off abruptly and said: "I know all about it, and I read in the paper that you talked to him about his play The Respectful Prostitute. *I've also been told that the municipality asked you to participate in the reception for Arthur Miller.... But what has this got to do with our topic? Sartre isn't a poet. Arthur Miller has absolutely nothing to do with poetry and poets. And even if this French existentialist had* been a poet, and the late Marilyn Monroe's husband had written poetry, what has that got to do with listening to your nonsense? I've come here to forget about my troubles and rest after a hard day's work.... My friend, I don't feel like listening! But let's get it over with ..."

I paid him his lacquered wooden camel, and he put it in his pocket and listened grudgingly as I read him my latest poem.

One day I said to my friend: "OK ... And what do you have to say about the Hebrew poet Natan Zach and his splendid beard? He came here with a writer-friend of his from Paris and bought a camel from me to give to his French guest ..." My friend cut me off and said: "I don't see any connection between a great poet like Zach and you." And I quickly shut him up with the usual camel ... which he put in his pocket, and then, without looking at me or offering any visible sign that he was paying attention to the words, he listened to the new poem I'd written the previous night.

Mostly I was afraid that the ongoing blackmail would use up all of my "capital" and one day empty the store, and I'd end up with neither camels to sell to the tourists nor anyone to listen to my poems.

Last week, to my great surprise, I was sent a Spanish literary journal with poems by Natan Zach and Taha Muhammad Ali on facing pages. And that same week I also received an invitation to participate in the International Poetry Festival in Jerusalem. I took the Spanish journal and the invitation, and went to my friend and told him: What do you have to say now? Natan Zach and I in the same magazine! And this is an invitation to read at a festival where hundreds of people will hear my poems, including agents and journalists and people from television.

My friend took my hand between both his palms and looked at me directly with both his eyes and said: "Taha, you're a wonderful poet! I tried to burn you to a crisp! I told myself: 'If there's anything left after I've burned him, then he's a real poet. But if *he's lost in the clamor of the street, and transformed entirely into ash and dust blown by the winds, then there's no need to feel sorry for him, no need to be sad about what he's written.' And thus, my friend, I took part in your creation!"*

The following day, my friend came to me carrying a fairly large cardboard box and said: "And these, my dear friend, are your camels!! Safe and sound and yours once again!"

*

Taha Muhammad Ali entered the shop, his head rising ponderously above a sharply stooped back. A large, clownish nose and jutting jaw suggested the uneasy cohabitation of mirth and menace. Three parallel furrows ran up from brow to crown in a face whose raw, impacted vitality might have been painted by Francis Bacon. He shook my hand vigorously before proposing that we drive to his home, located in one of the neighborhoods of Nazareth. I soon found myself sitting on the balcony of a two-story stone house surrounded by densely planted fruit trees—a concentrated version of the traditional Arab *bustan*—and by rosebushes and a huge scarlet bougainvillea that rambled over the porch. Ali's home seemed to belong to another time and place in the generally bleak mix of debris-strewn lots, pitted roads, and unfinished cinderblock homes, some rising to four or five stories. The neighborhood had seen better days, as its Arabic name, Bir el-Amir, "The Prince's Well," suggested. Like most Arab neighborhoods, villages, and towns in Israel, Bir el-Amir suffered from overcrowding, a paucity of state-allocated municipal funds, and neglect.

It was here that we met, sporadically over the next few years, sitting on Ali's balcony, or, come winter, in the reception room adjoining his living room, to converse, in a mixture of English, Hebrew, and Arabic. But mostly I listened to the poet's animated, impassioned talk. Ali was a born raconteur, and his talk—of his childhood in Saffuriya, of his early years selling trinkets from a peddler's cart, of his visit to Lebanon in 1983 to meet a childhood sweetheart now living in a refugee camp—tended to spill over into poetry. Was this a poem or just another extempore story that I was hearing in the poet's excited accents? I was never quite sure. Ali's talk had a certain self-propelling quality to it, one which I soon realized charmed, baffled, and exasperated even the most fluent of Arabic speakers.

Saffuriya, or at least the village of his childhood, where myth and reality converged, shone in the poet's mind as a place of prelapsarian innocence and embodied, in Palestinian terms, that period before the "great catastrophe," *an-nakba,* brought about by the Arab–Israeli war of 1948 and the consequent shattering and exodus of the Palestinian community. In July of that year, Ali's village, which had sheltered local militiamen, was hit by artillery and then bombed by Israeli aircraft. Most of the villagers fled into the surrounding wadis and orchards, believing that the Arab Liberation Army would come to their defense. But the ALA was not forthcoming, and the inhabitants of Saffuriya dispersed. Some made their way northward, to Lebanon, while others found temporary refuge in the neighboring villages of Kufr Cana and Reine, whose inhabitants were soon driven out as well, this time in the direction of Nazareth. The poet and his family chose the northern route to Lebanon, where they spent a year in a refugee camp before managing to infiltrate back into Israel. By then, however, the IDF had leveled Saffuriya to the ground, and the Israeli authorities had handed over to local kibbutzim thousands of dunams of fertile village land. Like many other former inhabitants of Saffuriya, Ali and his family settled in Nazareth, where he has remained for the last fifty years.

During one of my visits the poet drove me to what was left of Saffuriya, now called Tzippori (derived from the noun "bird" in Hebrew and spoken Arabic). Only five kilometers northwest of Nazareth, situated on a wooded rise and surrounded by vast stretches of cultivated fields, traces of the village, which once boasted some four thousand Muslim inhabitants, were barely discernible in a few cactus hedges and tumbledown stone terraces. Tzippori is now a thriving *moshav*, or Jewish farming community. Ali casually pointed from the window of his car at a couple of large, broken stones near some wild bramble bushes outside the driveway of a handsome, whitewashed villa: "Our home was here," he said, and drove on. I cast a backward glance at the village and, further up, at the archeological site of Sepphoris, inhabited at one time or another by Canaanites, Persians, Greeks, Romans, Jews, Byzantines, Crusaders, and Muslims. The site had recently become a major tourist attraction, after magnificent mosaic floors were uncovered in what had been a Roman villa. The Ottoman Sultan Abdul Hamid's citadel, which had served as a schoolhouse during Ali's childhood, rose above the dusty shrubbery. Then dusk descended as we wound up the hills leading into Nazareth, the song of blackbirds rising from the darkening orchards behind us.

*

Perhaps because the poet is an autodidact whose formal education ended in 1948—he had a family to support, and lived, like the entire Israeli-Arab community, under martial law until 1966—the poetry came slowly. He describes the late fifties and sixties as a time when he would sell souvenirs to the Christian tourists during the day and study classical Arabic texts in the evening: the pre-Islamic *Mu'allaqat*, or "Suspended Odes," *Kitab al-Aghani* (The Book of Songs), Al-Mutanabbi, Abu-Nuwas, the Andalusian Ibn Quzman, *A Thousand and One Nights*, and twentieth-century writers Taha Hussein, Kahlil Gibran, Badr Shakir Al-Sayyab, Adonis, Nizar Qabbani, Fadwa Touqan, and especially the Syrian Muhammad Al-Maghut, who was, like Ali, self-educated. Ali was also reading the English Romantic poets and, in Arabic translation, Chekhov, Maupassant, and Poe. He published his first short stories in the fifties, long before publishing poetry. But by the early seventies, when his poetry began appearing in various Arabic periodicals, in Israel and abroad, the poet's tiny, unassuming souvenir shop on Casanova Street had become an informal meeting place for such leading literary figures as Michel Haddad, Jamal Qawar, Samih Al-Qasim, and the near-legendary Rashid Hussein—schoolteacher, journalist, translator, and poet. (Persecuted by both Arabs and Israelis for his belief in co-existence—he translated into Arabic Israel's first national poet, H. N. Bialik, and, into Hebrew, together with Natan Zach, a collection of Palestinian folk poems—Hussein died, impoverished and alcoholic, in 1977, in a fire in his New York City apartment, where he had lived in exile since the late sixties.)

Ali absorbed the lessons of the European- and American–influenced "free-verse movement" which burgeoned in the fifties in Lebanon and Iraq. The Beirut-based *Shi'r* magazine had become at the time the standard-bearer for a new poetry, advocating at once prosodic experimentation, literary and political engagement, and the interpretation of contemporary themes through the rediscovery of myths indigenous to the Middle East. Great emphasis was placed by poets such as Yusuf al-Khal and Adonis (Ali Ahmad Sa'id) on the idea of renewal, or, in archetypal terms, of rejuvenation—of death and rebirth as exemplified, for instance, in the Tammuz fertility myth—and Palestine became a living symbol of a land turned barren that one day would become fertile again.

Dispossession, exile, and cultural marginilization—the sine qua non of Palestinian poetry, especially that written in the Arab diaspora—more often than not were treated symbolically, or even allegorically, and the figure of the Palestinian took on heroic dimensions (he was likened to Sinbad the Sailor, Ulysses, Harun al-Rashid, Lazarus, Houdini). Ali's poetry, by contrast, eschews the heroic mode and is set in the context of everyday experience. His only semi-mythological figure, Abd El-Hadi the Fool, is an innocent dreamer "who gets on my anger's nerves / and lights the fuse of my folly." This doesn't mean that political and historical events are glossed over, but rather that feelings of collective humiliation, shame, rage, and disillusionment (augmented not only by the June war of 1967 and the Israeli invasion of Lebanon in 1982, but by the repeated sense of betrayal by the Arab world) are modified by a highly individualized voice grounded in the history and language of the Galilee, and tempered by the work of memory and the imagination.

The singularity of Ali's poetry, and particularly his use of Arabic, needs some elaboration. Arabic poetry may have freed itself in the last half century from the trammels of an excessively formalized verse and absorbed a wide range of modern techniques—from the high symbolism of *The Waste Land*, to the radical disjunctions of French Surrealism—but it has also remained, on the whole, loyal in its use of *fusḥa* (literally, pure) or classical Arabic, as well as in its tendency to favor a high over a low diction. Every educated Arab child, in essence, grows up with two semi-independent linguistic systems: one spoken and particular to the region in which he lives, and the other written, rooted in the Qur'an, and consequently pan-Arabic. A Syrian visiting Morocco might have a hard time making himself understood in the souk of Casablanca, but he will have no difficulty reading the local paper. Newspapers, the news on television, academic texts, philosophical tracts, novels, poetry, are all written, for the most part, in *fusḥa*—a literary language of great lexical and syntactic richness, but also one that is inherently conservative. Its venerable rhetorical tradition and inflationary allure has not diminished to this day. Hence the very real difficulty in writing an anti-rhetorical poetry that would transcend the layers of literary convention that poets traditionally manipulate. There is, in fact, something quietly subversive in deflating the language of declamation and reverting to a poetics of essences, which is at once innocent of pomp and cunning in craft. "For an Arab poet to be truly modern," writes Adonis, "his writing must glow like a flame which rises from the fire of the ancient, but at the same time is entirely new."

This is not to say that attempts to use colloquial speech in poetry and fiction haven't been made. Individual poets and writers, among them the Egyptian Salah Abd Al-Sabur and the Syrian Nizar Qabbani, have experimented with dialect and the local vernacular, and with rhythms that approximate the rhythms of common speech. But this has been done with caution and, in order to legitimize their deviations from a purely literary idiom, poets have often drawn on the traditional colloquial *zajal*, a form, by and large satirical in nature, whose master was the twelfth-century Ibn Quzman. Until very recently the use of the colloquial in poetry has been associated, at best, with popular folk literature and traditional songs, and, at worst, with the actual corruption of the Arabic language. Naguib Mahfouz, for example, the Dickens of modern Arabic fiction, writes with considerable vehemence of his opposition to popular speech forms: "The colloquial is one of the diseases from which the people are suffering, and of which they are bound to rid themselves as they progress. I consider the colloquial one of the failings of our society, exactly like ignorance, poverty, and disease."

Ali writes a literary Arabic that incorporates or, as he puts it, "grafts" onto the classical forms, significant elements of a colloquial and often idiosyncratic Arabic. In contrast to the stylized diction of most of his contemporaries, spoken Palestinian Arabic of the central Galilee anchors the poetry to the page and endows it with specificity without ever sounding merely like dialect. Ali has therefore been perceived by some readers and critics as a popular, or *'amiyeh,* poet and story-teller whose poetry is removed from the strains of his younger Palestinian contemporaries, Samih al-Qasim and Mahmoud Darwish, both of whom write an engaged poetry of resistance in the most resonant tones of *fusha*–which in itself assures them an audience inside and outside of Israel, the West Bank, Gaza, and Jordan. But Ali's seeming insularity within the Palestinian community should not be disparaged. The poet and critic Na'im Araidi has pointed out that Ali's originality (and even his relevance to the Palestinian cause) lies precisely in his localized use of language, where the blending of the literary and the spoken, as well as the poet's sense of the natural, homespun image contribute to the poetry's apparent simplicity while belying all along its complex sensibility. Saffuriya may have been leveled to the ground, but its mores, language, and geography remain paradigms of durable hope in the poet's imagination. In effect Ali's poetry, and the groundedness of its language, constitute yet another means of clinging to his home and land, and of being, in Palestinian terms, a *samid*–a term coined by Palestinians in the late seventies, meaning one who holds on tenaciously to his land and its culture, and perseveres in adverse times.

*

Written in a forceful, direct style, in short lines of varying beats, with a minimum of fuss and a rich array of images drawn primarily from village life, Ali's poetry recalls in contemporary terms the work of the great modern Turkish poet, Nazim Hikmet, as well as the Central and Eastern European poetry of Ungaretti, of Holan, of Róewicz and Herbert, and of Weöres and Juhász, poets who wrote with unflinching honesty as the lights dimmed in their native lands. Such poets replaced the "poeticisms" of their elders with a stark, emotional directness. Montale spoke of wanting to "wring the neck of the eloquence of our old aulic language, even at the risk of a counter-eloquence," a turn of phrase which seems particularly applicable to Ali's own poetics. But the poet's spoken rhythms and lean diction also suggests the down-to-earth vitality and inventiveness of America's early modernist poets. William Carlos Williams comes to mind: "And in proportion as a man has bestirred himself to become awake to his own locality he will perceive more and more of what is disclosed and find himself in a position to make the necessary translations. The disclosures will then and only then come to him as reality, as joy, as release."

Ali has bestirred himself awake, and in doing so he has released a complex of emotions of startling and often unexpected force. One may be charmed by the poet himself, the village chronicler and seller of trinkets, the self-educated poet who has described himself as "a camel fleeing the slaughterhouses / galloping toward the East, / pursued by processions / of knives and assessors, / women wielding / mortar and pestle for chop meat!" But the parallel thrust of Ali's work is revealed in a harsh, often painful realism, in emotional desolation, and in telling images of desertion, ruin, and the sudden eruption of violence that act as a foil to any temptation to give in to mere folklore and nostalgia. Not infrequently pain, joy, bitterness, and hope are inexorably linked, as in "The Evening Wine of Aged Sorrow," or in the poet's marvelous story, "So What," where a child's walking barefoot for the first ten years of his life leads to cuts and scars from "daggers of splintered glass," and "thorns sharp as venomous stingers," but also to the unmediated, tactile exploration of his surroundings:

> ... I'd walk, stand, and then walk in the water which usually covered my calf muscle, feeling against my bare legs and the flesh of my feet and the nerve-ends of my toes small pieces of metal, for the most part little coins with holes at their center, coins that had been lost by their owners and swept up by the water, or marbles, bullet casings, and old ladies' copper rings which had been thrown away by grandsons, and small keys, and sometimes bigger keys, in addition to crooked old nails, bent like the words of liars.

It is hard to think of another Palestinian poet of Ali's generation who writes with such intimacy while skillfully modulating between the personal and the public spheres of life. Ali speaks in what might be called a figurative plainness, reducing the traditional rhetorical flourishes of Arabic literature to a minimum.

In "Empty Words," for example, he addresses his "little notebook / yellow as a spike of wheat," in a tone reminiscent of Waller as echoed in early Pound. Though here, too, pastoral fancy soon turns into unremitting and even brutal sorrow—a sorrow that is at once private and communal as the poet alludes to the exodus of Palestinians from the Haifa seaport in 1948. The poetry may be acutely personal, but time after time it conveys the sense that happiness is not something that "flees / every which way / like a partridge." It is of another order altogether, and must in the end ally itself to the aesthetic realm, and the natural world embodied in the Blakean "minute particulars" of Saffuriya. Lightened by a touch of the trickster's wiles (*Fooling the Killers* is the title of the poet's second volume of poems) the poetry is at once lyrical and blunt, graceful and harsh in its veracities.

*

Invited once again to Jerusalem to read from his work in the spring of 1997, Taha Muhammad Ali prefaced his poems with another short tale. (Introducing his poems with a story, the poet explained, was like watching the animated trailers that used to be run before a feature film appeared on the screen.) This time the poet spoke not of wooden camels but of an old-fashioned mousetrap. The story went something like this: One day, back in 1941, Ali's mother discovered a mouse in their home. She gave her son two piasters and told him to run off to the local shopkeeper in Saffuriya and buy a mousetrap. Ali returned with the mousetrap, which the shopkeeper had mentioned was rare and made only in Hebron, and at exactly five o'clock he heard the trap door click shut. "I then saw," the poet exclaimed, his wrinkles creasing in his troll-like face, "the most beautiful mouse, with green eyes and a belly white as cotton." Fifty years later, the poet's wife spotted a mouse in her Nazareth kitchen and implored her husband, "Taha, quick, fetch me a mousetrap." Ali drove into Nazareth and was told that the sort of mousetrap he was looking for no longer existed, though someone had heard that they were still being made in Hebron, now part of the West Bank. A week later, it just so happened, the poet was scheduled to read his poems at the Hebron Sports Club. Ali recited his poems and was then invited to a sumptuous lunch. At the conclusion of the meal he asked his new friends, "By the way, does anyone in Hebron sell old-fashioned mousetraps?" A young man said that he knew where they could be purchased, and promptly drove the poet to one of the local stores where Ali saw the exact same mousetrap he had bought for two piasters as a child. "Did you make these traps?" he asked the owner of the shop. "No," the man answered, "they were made by my father, Ziab Al-Shantawi." Ali paused, and then said to the Jerusalem crowd: "This was the very same name as the shopkeeper in Saffuriya." And so he returned home with a new-old mousetrap, and the next day, he added, at exactly five o'clock the mousetrap clicked shut, and once more he saw "the same, beautiful mouse, with green eyes and a belly white as cotton ..."

The audience of Israelis—and a handful of Palestinians—chuckled, uneasily perhaps, and somewhat beguiled, for all were now dislocated: aware that the poet had caught them in the snare of his words, though it was hard to know just how. Ali, too, was visibly shaken by the story, as Saffuriya of half a century ago was suddenly, disturbingly present, while present and future seemed every bit as fragile as the past he had summoned to his poems.

Gabriel Levin

ABD EL-HADI FIGHTS A SUPERPOWER

In his life
he neither wrote nor read.
In his life he
didn't cut down a single tree,
didn't slit the throat
of a single calf.
In his life he did not speak
of the *New York Times*
behind its back,
didn't raise
his voice to a soul
except in his saying:
"Come in, please,
by God, you can't refuse."

*

Nevertheless—
his case is hopeless,

his situation
desperate.
His God-given rights are a grain of salt
tossed into the sea.

Ladies and gentlemen of the jury:
about his enemies
my client knows not a thing.
And I can assure you,
were he to encounter
the entire crew
of the aircraft carrier *Enterprise,*
he'd serve them eggs
sunny side up,
and labneh
fresh from the bag.

VII.73

POST-OPERATIVE COMPLICATIONS
FOLLOWING THE EXTRACTION OF MEMORY

In an ancient, gypsy
dictionary of dreams
are explanations of my name
and numerous
interpretations of all I'll write.

What horror comes across me
when I come across myself
in such a dictionary!
But there I am:
a camel fleeing the slaughterhouses,
galloping toward the East,
pursued by processions
of knives and assessors,
women wielding
mortar and pestle for chop meat!

I do not consider myself a pessimist,
and I certainly don't

suffer from the shock
of ancient, gypsy nightmares,
and yet, in the middle of the day,
whenever I turn on the radio,
or turn it off,
I breathe in a kind of historical,
theological leprosy.

Feeling the bonds of language
coming apart in my throat and loins,
I cease attending
to my sacred obligations:
barking, and the gnashing of teeth.

I confess!
I've been neglecting
my post-operative physiotherapy
following the extraction of memory.
I've even forgotten
the simplest way of collapsing
in exhaustion on the tile floor.

10.IV.73

THROMBOSIS IN THE VEINS OF PETROLEUM

When I was a child
I fell into the abyss
but didn't die;
I drowned in the pond
when I was young,
but did not die;
and now, God help us—
one of my habits is running
into battalions of land mines
along the border,
as my songs
and the days of my youth
are dispersed:
here a flower,
there a scream;
and yet,
I do not die!

*

They butchered me
on the doorstep
like a lamb for the feast—
thrombosis
in the veins of petroleum;
In God's name
they slit my throat
from ear to ear
a thousand times,
and each time
my dripping blood would swing
back and forth
like the feet of a man
hanged from a gallows,
and come to rest,
a large, crimson mallow
blossom—
a beacon
to guide ships
and mark
the site of palaces
and embassies.

*

And tomorrow,
God help us—
the phone won't ring
in a brothel or castle,
and not in a single Gulf Emirate,
except to offer a new prescription
for my extermination.
But ...
just as the mallow tells us,
and as the borders know,
I won't die! I will not die!!
I'll linger on—a piece of shrapnel
the size of a penknife
lodged in the neck;
I'll remain—
a blood stain
the size of a cloud
on the shirt of this world!

23.IX.73

CRACK IN THE SKULL

The town shut down
the day the school
guardian died.
Women's breasts went soft,
and the people went to sleep
in the late afternoon,
so great was their grief.

*

The doctor was summoned
and gave his full attention
to the stomach and brain,
wiped the blood
from the collar,
extracted ash-gray
samples from his pockets
and passed them out
among the members

of his family
like sweetmeats on Thursdays.

He was eulogized by a man
with bushy eyebrows, and a fan,
who works as a drummer.
The words he spoke in his praise
brought the swallows down
from the seventh heaven,
and made one's pills
thick in the throat.

He mentioned the primary
causes of death:
a crack in the Byzantine inscriptions
lining the walls of the skull,
tumescence in the dextral
Latin clause,
fatigue, hunger, vagrancy,
debts and addiction to ruin.
Even the owner of the cemetery
thought about Death

once again: he spat at the world
and offered the grave free of charge.
The head guard fainted.
There's nothing like a catastrophe
to bring a graveyard attendant
back to his mother tongue.

The poor soul
sobbed in Armenian:
"I'll protect you,
son of God's servant,
I'll protect you from the crows
and the spotted hyenas."

             *

On his headstone they chiseled
themes for a composition
brought from distant lands
in a horse-drawn wagon.
They imposed a curfew,
and took him around
from wasteland to swamp,

so the Lord
would know him by heart.

1.VIII.71

WARNING

Lovers of hunting,
and beginners seeking your prey:
Don't aim your rifles
at my happiness,
which isn't worth
the price of the bullet
(you'd waste on it).
What seems to you
so nimble and fine,
like a fawn,
and flees
every which way,
like a partridge,
isn't happiness.
Trust me:
my happiness bears
no relation to happiness.

12.IX.88

FOOLING THE KILLERS

Qasim,
I wonder now
where you are....
I haven't forgotten you
after all these years,
long as the graveyard
wall is long. I always
ask the grass of the field
about you, and the dirt paths.

Are you alive,
with your poise,
your cane, and memories?
Did you marry?
Do you have a tent of your own,
and children?
Did you make it to Mecca?
Or did they kill you
at the foot of the Hill of Tin?

Or maybe you never grew up,
Qasim, and managed to hide,
behind your mere ten years,
and you're still the same old Qasim,
the boy who runs around
and laughs
and jumps over fences,
who likes green almonds
and searches for birds' nests.

But even if they did it,
Qasim,
if, shamelessly,
they killed you,
I'm certain
you fooled your killers,
just as you managed
to fool the years.
For they never discovered
your body at the edge of the road,
and didn't find it
where the rivers spill,
or on the shelves

at the morgue,
and not on the way to Mecca,
and not beneath the rubble.

As no one saw you
concealing your corpse,
so no one will ever set eyes on you,
and no earthly breeze
encounter a bone of your body,
a finger of your hand,
or even a single shoe
that might fit you.
Qasim, you fooled them.

*

I always envied you, Qasim,
your skill at hiding
in the games of hide-and-seek we played—
barefoot at dusk—forty years ago—
when we were little boys.

28.VIII.88

EXODUS

The street is empty
as a monk's memory,
and faces explode in the flames
like acorns—
and the dead crowd the horizon
and doorways.
No vein can bleed
more than it already has,
no scream will rise
higher than it's already risen.
We will not leave!
Everyone outside is waiting
for the trucks and the cars
loaded with honey and hostages.
We will not leave!
The shields of light are breaking apart
before the rout and the siege;
outside, everyone wants us to leave.
But we will not leave!

Ivory white brides
trail their veils
in captivity's glare, waiting,
and everyone outside wants us to leave,
but we will not leave!
The big guns pound the jujube groves,
destroying the dreams of the violets,
extinguishing the bread, killing the salt,
unleashing thirst
and parching lips and souls.
And everyone outside is saying:
"What are we waiting for?
Warmth we're denied,
the air itself has been seized—
Why aren't we leaving?"

Masks fill the pulpits and brothels,
the places of ablution.
Masks cross-eyed with utter amazement;
they do not believe what is now so clear,
and fall, astonished
and writhing like worms or like tongues.

We will not leave!
Are we in this inside only to leave?
Leaving is just for the masks, for the pulpits
and conferences.
Leaving is just
for the siege-that-comes-from-within,
the siege that comes from the Bedouin's loins,
the siege of the brethren
inflicted by the taste of the sword's blade
and the stink of crows.
We will not leave!

Outside they're blocking the exits
and offering their blessings
to the imposter,
praying, petitioning
Almighty God for our deaths.

5.II.83

AMBERGRIS

Our traces have all been erased,
our impressions swept away—
and all the remains
have decayed ...
there isn't a single sign
left to guide us
or show us a thing.
The age has grown old,
the days long,
and I, if not for the lock of your hair,
auburn as the nectar of carob,
and soft as the scent of silk
that was here before,
dozing like Arabian jasmine,
shimmering like the gleam of dawn,
pulsing like a star—
I, if not for that lock of camphor,
would feel not a thing
linking me to this land.

This land is a traitor
and can't be trusted.
This land doesn't remember love.
This land is a whore
holding out a hand to the years,
as it manages a ballroom
on the harbor pier—
it laughs in every language
and bit by bit, with its hip,
feeds all who come to it.

This land denies,
cheats and betrays us;
we're too much for it;
it grumbles about us—
detests us.
Its newcomers,
sailors and usurpers,
uproot the backyard gardens,
burying the trees.

They keep us from looking too long
at the anemone blossom and cyclamen,
and won't allow us to touch the herbs,
the wild artichoke and chicory.

*

Our land makes love to the sailors
and strips naked before the newcomers;
it rests its head along the usurpers' thigh,
is disgraced and defiled in its sundry accents;
there seems to be nothing that would bind it to us,
and I—if not for the lock of your hair,
auburn as the nectar of carob,
and soft as the scent of silk,
if not for the camphor,
if not for the musk and the sweet basil,
and if not for the ambergris—
I would not know it,
and would not love it,
and would not go near it ...

*

Your braid
is the only thing
linking me, like a noose, to this whore.

10.III.83

THE EVENING WINE OF AGED SORROW

At dusk,
as day is crushed
like a skull,
time collapses
like towering bridges
or vaults,
moments scatter
like shattered glass
from a car crash—
and despair
suddenly appears,
doubts gather,
fears are freed,
and worries stretch out their necks,
sharpened
like the heads of scorpions.

At dusk
sadness burgeons,

increases with every breath,
stirs with every memory,
and with each wave of longing
swells and blossoms.
At dusk a sensation
of darkness and gloom
floods the chest—
amassing like silt,
closing in
like a wall—
it tightens around one's neck,
assaults the veins,
slowly creeps like clouds
burdened with weariness,
like countless blinded birds
that have lost their way
to the heart of the forest.
And it seems, Amira,
the birds and rivers as well recall
their homeland at dusk.

And through the pleasant desert winter,

which fills one's heart and memory
with silk and buds,
I see the ardor of birds,
the yearning of rivers,
catch sight of the flocks
of emptiness, hollow
as the hole of a cellar.
I witness the calamity
of the sundials in retreat,
like ships that have lost
track of their ports—
or armies,
that have lost their leaders
and supply of water.

*

As for you, my captive
olive tree,
a splendid evening to you,
my tree of enduring captivity,
branches of the everlasting journey,

wounds of the endless wandering—
your moistened eyelids
remind me of them,
your defeated shadow
recalls for me
my father.
O ... Father,
if only you were alive,
still chewing your bitterness
and waiting,
angry, coughing,
and wearing your robe,
as you would.
I'd complain to you
of this wretched sadness
which pierces my chest each evening
like a sword forged in burning coals,
like a river carved out of stone.

                    *

And, nevertheless,
ever since

I first caressed
the air of this world
with the tips of my fingers—
I've been dreaming ...
dreaming of flowers
warm as the eyes of children,
dreaming of streets and forests
that cover the slopes and seasons
and cross the garden of the hours
and seep through spontaneous space
made of stars and spikes of wheat,
a place where the evening
would smile at me,
leaning over to offer me comfort
like the gentlest of grandfathers,
before it disperses
behind the tumult
of caravans of spices and wine.

             *

What feelings
of sad and precious joy

come across me,
when I see the evening
weeping softly, and mercifully,
as though with the tears of sisters,
which soon vanish
like the last breaths
taken by pellets of hail.

24.V.83

THREE QASIDAS

I. Imprisonment
When I was free,
my fear was wrapped
around my neck
like a viper!
And you were the sole
spring of my sadness.

But now ...
the bread of my fear has been depleted
and the wine of my sorrow
pours forth from every fountain.

II. Release
When I was a prisoner,
nights were heavy
as lead
and the stillness was hard

as a millstone.
The stone pressed down against the lead,
and the lead was ground,
but the lead didn't dissolve,
and the millstone didn't crumble.
And you were my refuge.

But now ...
What saqi
has mingled the night with stillness
without killing silence,
or murdering loneliness?

III. The Dream
Once
I'd see you departing
in the dream,
and sorrow would take
hold in my throat,
and because it was only a dream,
I'd wake

and be happy ...
and fields of wheat would fill the day.
And you were that sorrow,
and you were that joy.

But now ...
I dream you are coming
and I'm happy,
and wake to discover
it was only a dream,
and so the sorrow
wells up in my throat,
and dusk is covered with thorns.

20.VIII.88

MAYBE

Last night in my dream
I saw I would die.
I saw death eye to eye
and felt it—
was there inside it.
The truth is— I've never known
that death through most of its stages
would flow so easily:
a white, warm,
wide and pleasant torpor,
a soothing sensation of lethargy.

Generally speaking,
there was neither pain nor fear;
maybe our excessive fear
of death is rooted
in an intense
escalation of desire for life.
Maybe.

But in my death
the one thing
I can't describe
is the sudden shiver
that comes across us
when we know for certain we're dying,
that soon our loved ones will vanish,
that we will not see them ever again,
or even be able to think of them.

22.III.88

EMPTY WORDS

Ah, little notebook,
yellow as a spike of wheat
and still as a face,
I've protected you
from dampness and rodents
and entrusted you with
my sadness and fear,
and my dreams—
though I've gotten from you
only disobedience and betrayal ...

For otherwise where are the words
which would have me saying:
If only I were a rock on a hill ...
unable to see or hear,
be sad or suffer!
And where is the passage
whose tenor is this:

I wish I could be
a rock on a hill
which the young men
from Hebron explode
and offer as a gift to Jerusalem's children,
ammunition for their palms and slings!

And where is the passage
in which I wanted
to be a rock on a hill
gazing out from on high
hundreds of years from now
over hordes
of masked liberators!

And where is what belongs
to my dream of being
a rock on a hill
along the Carmel?
Where will I call on the source of my sadness,
gazing out over the waves
and thinking of her

to whom I bade
farewell at the harbor pier
in Haifa forty years ago,
and still ...
I await her return
one evening
with the doves of the sea.

*

Is it fair, little notebook,
yellow as a spike of wheat
and still as a face,
that you conceal
what you cancel and erase,
simply because it consists
of empty words—
which frighten no enemy
and offer no hope to a friend?

4.IX.88

TWIGS

Neither music
fame nor wealth,
not even poetry itself,
could provide consolation
for life's brevity,
or the fact that *King Lear*
is a mere eighty pages long, and comes to an end,
and for the thought that one might suffer greatly
on account of a rebellious child.

*

My love for you
is what's magnificent,
but I, you, and the others,
most likely,
are ordinary people.

*

My poem
goes beyond poetry
because you
exist
beyond the realm of women.

*

And so
it has taken me
all of sixty years
to understand
that water is the finest drink,
and bread the most delicious food,
and that art is worthless
unless it plants
a measure of splendor in people's hearts.

*

After we die,
and the weary heart
has lowered its final eyelid
on all that we've done,
and on all that we've longed for,
on all that we've dreamt of,
all we've desired
or felt,
hate will be
the first thing
to putrefy
within us.

1989–1991

THE HEIGHT OF LOVE

What makes me love
being alive
is something I can't quite describe,
or put into words with my pen
or utter aloud....
I love the world, and dreams
set in that forest of light
on the banks of the mystery
of my shameful ignorance
(concerning
the boat's destination
and the journey's goal)
—that at which
I haven't dared
hint or point ...

And even if
the days were emptied
of all that was finer

of all that was finer
than the reed-flute's rasp,
of all that is more desirable
than the warmth of the winter's fire,
even if they were emptied
of all that is sweeter
than "How are you?"
wafting up
from a winning smile,
I would go on
preferring life
to a thousand deaths!

However,
my enemies' tragedy
owes all to their rush
to rehearse my death—
as a thief is impatient
to get
to his specious prayers.
They do not grasp
why

I spend my spirit
like counterfeit coins,
or how I could leave my blood behind

... and decades, decades
of delectation and love—
how could I shed them
for the sake of what I love?

10.VIII.89

SABHA'S ROPE

Do you remember, Abu Muhammad,
do you remember when Sabha,
our neighbor Abu Hashem's cow,
swallowed the rope?
Do you remember how,
as she was dying,
they slaughtered her,
and, by lamp light,
flayed her and then,
bit by bit, with axes,
hacked her into pieces?

Um Hashem
sent up her wailing,
as the knives sliced
away at Sabha,
and her daughter wept.
Everyone grieved,
and everyone lent a hand,

insisting, "We'll share the burden.
We'll manage."

The villagers
rushed together,
shoulder to shoulder,
without exception
to buy Sabha's meat!
Do you remember—
or have you fallen asleep?

No, I'm awake,
of course I remember,
and I remember, too,
that no one ever
tasted a piece of that meat!

It was grilled,
fried, cooked,
and minced for chop meat,
but no one ate it!
The people felt

they were slicing into flesh
fresh from a cadaver,
as though it were Abu Hashem's body,
or that of his family,
that was being carved.
Men and women turned in disgust
and threw it away.

For a while,
the village was choked
in a muted sort of grief,
like Abu Hashem's hoarse voice,
and green as Sabha's eyes.
Don't you see, Abu Muhammad,
our village was pleasant.
It's true, there were hard times,
but the bitterness was good,
like chicory,
or better!
You see what I mean ...
wasn't it pleasant?

—Pleasant?!
Ha! ...
Pleasant, he says, ... pleasant.
Let me tell you,
by the book of Almighty Allah,
I swear to you,
I was prepared,
in fact I would have preferred,
and with all my heart I would have agreed,
to swallow a rope longer than Sabha's,
if only
we could have stayed in our village.

15.III.88

MEETING AT AN AIRPORT

You asked me once,
on our way back
from the midmorning
trip to the spring:
"What do you hate,
and *who* do you love?"

And I answered,
from behind the eyelashes
of my surprise,
my blood rushing
like the shadow
cast by a cloud of starlings:
"I hate departure ...
I love the spring
and the path to the spring,
and I worship the middle
hours of morning."
And you laughed ...

and the almond tree blossomed
and the thicket grew loud with nightingales.

... A question
now four decades old:
I salute that question's answer;
and an answer,
as old as your departure;
I salute that answer's question ...

And today,
it's preposterous,
here we are at a friendly airport
by the slimmest of chances,
and we meet.
Ah, Lord!
we meet.
And here you are
asking—again,
it's absolutely preposterous—
I recognized you
but you didn't recognize me.

"Is it you?!"
But you wouldn't believe it.
And suddenly
you burst out and asked:
"If you're really you,
What do you hate
and *who* do you love?!"

And I answered—
my blood
fleeing the hall,
rushing in me
like the shadow
cast by a cloud of starlings:
"I hate departure ...
and I love the spring
and the path to the spring,
and I worship the middle
hours of morning."

And you wept,
and flowers bowed their heads,
and doves in the silk of their sorrow stumbled.

NEVER MIND

Grandfather,
old hunter,
in your face I read only goodness,
though I, at your age,
refrained
from hunting the evening quail,
and when I had your vigor
I'd turn away
from the snake as it shed its pale sheath,
and say:
"Never mind."

     *

I'll feed your mangy dog.
I'll bring you tobacco and water.
I won't alarm the gazelles
or the wild doves
or say a word to the local inspectors.

The brotherhood of knives
hanging from belts
binds us in our search for fledgling partridges
in pockets and underneath hats.
My comrade in thirst,
lamenting the rabbits
in their innocence,
who leave to the righteous
no heart of purity—
I implore you:

Let me stroll
within range of your rifle,
among these deserted gardens
and ruined stone walls;
allow me
to greet this fig tree!
Let me draw near
to that particular cactus.
And then, after the harvest,
catch me
and slaughter me

with the fine threads
that dangle
from your sleeves and pack
like the guts from a chicken's belly!

13.IX.88

THIS IS THE COLLAPSING STEEL MIHRAB, AND THAT'S MY MOTHER, BEFORE SHE CEASED TO MOURN

Now I emerge from a nightmare
in which a naked hyena
with a striped face and muzzle
raped Fouzeeya,
our neighbor's daughter.

Her father stands there
grinning by her side,
and behind him there hovers a maidenly jinn—
hanging by her hair
from a collapsing steel mihrab.

I wake, my throat dry
as a nutshell,
my lips sealed,
I long to flee my future,
as sleep flees from the brow's balcony.

God, lock this away from us.
Lord, lock it away.

*

Certainly those who suckled us
were more optimistic than we are.
My mother, for instance:
if only her capacity for mourning
came back to her, she would heal me,
sweeping away all my fears
with a single, warm utterance:
"It'll be fine, my dear,
it's a good dream.
God bless our prophet Muhammad,
and you, Master Badawy,
please, make it good."

ABD EL-HADI THE FOOL

Before the dough of my skull was ravaged
by the buzzards of the world,
I was a fool!
I was naive ...
and wanted to fly;
I loved horses and poetry.
I dreamed of a meal
that would last forever,
drawn from the wonders
of Jaudar's saddlebags,
a feast from *A Thousand
and One Nights.*
I was a fool!

But after the rape
of the light of morning's laughter,
suddenly,
hatred filled me.
After the springs were buried alive,

after the vaults' destruction,
the flame swept through me.
After the pillaging of the shadow
and the sundering of the spikes of wheat ...
after the murder of the doves ...
I was charged with a sharpened hatred,
blue as the edge of death itself!

*

I'm no longer a fool,
and bitterness has settled
inside my soul.

Therefore ...
I'm about to explode:
retreating into my night,
my blood boiling ...

I wanted to burn down the world!
Wanted to stab it
in its soft belly,

and see it dismembered
after I'd drowned it.
And I vowed
I would not grant its face
the dignity
of a final farewell
at its burial....

Seas of heavy darkness
have drifted by,
and I am waiting.
Mountains of night have crept away,
and still I am waiting.
Ages, sluggish
as the pulse of caverns,
drag on,
and I lower my eyelashes
on the raging,
communing with it
and longing for bombers!

However,

my great apostasy
is this:
no sooner does the laughter
of a child reach me,
or I happen upon
a sobbing stream,
no sooner do I see
a flower wilting,
or notice a fine-looking woman,
than I'm stunned
and abandoned by everything,
and nothing of me remains
except
Abd El-Hadi the fool!

Abd El-Hadi
who gets on my anger's nerves
and lights the fuse of my folly,
as he unfurls his warm smile
embracing that very same world!
He shakes hands with creatures of various sorts;
embraces the righteous and wicked alike;

greets the victim and hangman as one.
The fool!
He hugs the world like a pillow;
he hugs the world as though it were
the memory of his own engagement ...
or a breeze coming across a field of wheat!
He takes the world to the hair of his chest
like his daughter ...
without there appearing on his face
any indication at all
that he's bothered
by the wailing,
by the sobbing,
by the tears
  flowing from the sockets of his eyes!

4.V.90

THE KID GOATS OF JAMIL

Jamil,
my father's cousin,
our neighbor in Saffuriya,
married three wives
but had from them
neither a son to inherit his name
nor a daughter to refresh his heart.

Jamil, my father's cousin,
our neighbor in Saffuriya,
owned a wide-eyed,
long-haired,
blonde Damascene she-goat
that gave birth to six wooly kid goats
two days after he returned from Mecca;
their silken breath reminded you
of the childhood
of the world!

Jamil's kid goats
are creatures of another world;
Jamil and his three wives' kid goats
are six dough-smooth figures of dawn,
six baby stars escaping
the nursery of a star-filled sky.
Their shadows won't stand still.

Stones sleep,
Satan sleeps,
shooting stars and fish sleep,
but Jamil's kid goats never tire.
The wind rests,
but Jamil's kid goats
never grow drowsy.

They scale the archway,
leap over the log pile,
scramble up to the roof's edge,
and run around in the courtyard,
then down the path
between the storeroom

and the goat shed.
Their frisky movements dissolve
their coats' gay colors.

Their craziness simply goes crazy
on evenings when the almonds go green
and with the return of the harvest moon.
The kid goats of Jamil and his wives
leap out of the windows of their skin.
They sway, pounce, and dance
in the silvery fullness of the world,
like dangling lamps of mercury
being tugged at by puppy-sized jinn.

The newly arrived kid goats
filled the hearts of Jamil and his wives
with a rare, buoyant joy;
they warmed their spirits
and spilled soft as velvet
into their home,
into the goat shed and onto the path,
perfuming the storeroom.

That joy was never limited
to the three wives;
that joy was never restricted
to the blonde, wide-eyed,
long-haired,
golden-hearted Damascene she-goat;
that joy was never confined to Jamil,
my father's cousin, our neighbor in Saffuriya.
A bright, hopeful joy
    spread out over the people,
        over the village,
    like the joy of the year's first rain.

SO WHAT

(1)

I went barefoot the first ten years of my life, and while I was bitter about being deprived of shoes, and my incessant desire to get hold of a pair overwhelmed me, my suffering on the day the Moroccan shoe salesman came to our village—on that day alone, by God—my suffering on that single day was such that it surpassed the torment I had suffered at having gone barefoot for the ten previous years combined.

(2)

But I should explain what I mean right away, lest one understand from this that my despair at having gone barefoot throughout the years that preceded the arrival of the Moroccan involved only fleeting, superficial feelings, free of any real misfortune or distress; for in fact, much as I try, I can barely begin to describe the damage done to me by the glances of the neighborhood boys, and the neighborhood men, and the neighborhood women, and even the glances aimed my way by young neighborhood girls who hadn't yet left the eggshell.

These looks from the children, in particular, struck with more power against my flesh and bones and blood, and burned more fiercely against my heart and spirit and nerves, than the hot embers of soil and sand beneath the soles of my feet in the scorching heat of summer. I'll never forget the words of our math teacher, who may have believed that my going barefoot was a kind of hobby I pursued with my father's encouragement—those words which in one way or another surfaced in the course of nearly every math lesson, words which, even at the height of summer, have always recalled for me the bite of frost-covered ground in the early hours of a winter day:

"What are we going to do with you, Khalid? Tell your father I'd like to see him. Tell him, for me, will you, a little manners wouldn't hurt."

All this, to say nothing of the thorns sharp as

venomous stingers, and the stones of the road and the paths, and the edges of the courtyard and threshing-floor pebbles pointed like the tips of nails ... and apart from the daggers of splintered glass, which carried out their skillful work on my feet, slicing, splitting, slashing as I played or jumped about, and as I raced around, now chasing my rivals and now running away from them. My mother would scream and scold me, especially as she took hot ashes from the oven or the brazier and applied them to a new and "serious" wound with which I'd just returned....

She'd wrap my injured foot in an old rag cut into strips from what once had been a piece of my sister Amneh's clothes—its color, as I remember it, once was green, and if it wasn't green, then most likely it was red. And then she would bind the rag with twine, tighter and tighter, till it held fast and I shrieked, the pain was so fierce. Mother would shout at me, her reproachful anger never entirely free of her sad and deep compassion, "You deserve it! You mischievous little boy. Haven't I told you a thousand times: Stop playing these games of yours."

"What can I do? I swear, I didn't see it.... I was on my way home ... a sharp piece of rusty iron stabbed me!"

(3)

No, this sense I had of being subject to an ordeal wasn't just fleeting and superficial; on the contrary, it made me miserable, and I was continually suffering on its account, always looking at shoes in the storefront windows and on other people's feet, despairing of ever getting hold of a pair of my own. I listened to the teacher's icy pearls of wisdom, and my teeth chattered; I gave in to the treatment for my wounds, to the hot ashes and the suffering, to absorbing the stares from behind me and before me and beside me, as I sunk into the bog of my agonizing shame. Oddest of all was the fact that the stares of the men and boys were one thing, but the stares of the girls were quite another. May God so love me that He one day allows me to return the favor to those skinny, little know-nothings who couldn't tell right from left, or the bleats of their mothers from the calls of the market fishmongers.

And so I would go into our house in the middle of a fiercely cold or unbearably hot day, and point to my two bare, swollen feet, redder than sore and bloodshot eyes. I would open my mouth, about to complain, my complaint paving the way for my request from my mother for a pound for shoes on sale in one of the storefront windows.... But I would soon understand that my arrival had interrupted a talk between my father and my mother—my father continuing on in his hoarse, lowered voice, and this before I could finish my complaint and find the words to ask for the money: "Like I told you, go to Abu Abbas, and tell him to sell it to us on credit. Tell him. He'll give you a two-piaster can of tomato paste.... He'll sell it to us on credit."

My mother would answer, pleading with him, "Please, you go, or send Khalid.... Here he is now ..."

I would swallow my complaint, gulp down my request, and shut my mouth on what suddenly seemed hotter than embers and more bitter even than wormwood.

All this is entirely true. But the truth of truths is also that what hurt me and made me miserable throughout these ten barefoot years came to a head on the day of the incident of that Moroccan's shoes. It was gathered, condensed, and intensified, added to and compounded, until it turned into a frightening nightmare that the mind cannot possibly envision or the imagination contain.... It aroused such mythical terror that day was turned into night for me, and the light was strewn with darkness, and sleep crept into my wakefulness. It happened in a single day, or more accurately, on just one afternoon of a single day, indeed I might say that it came into existence, took shape and revealed its power, like an explosion, within a single, distinct moment. My bitterness over not having had any shoes and my desire to acquire them were suddenly joined in a deep-seated burning that surpassed, in one brief instant, all I had suffered in the ten barefoot years combined.

The thing I remember now, and which seems so strange to me that I barely believe it happened, is that the incident didn't at first make much of an impression on me. It was of no special interest and aroused no unusual concern. I didn't stop running around when the boys I was playing with in the neighborhood after the afternoon prayers on that day began to spread the word: the wandering shoe salesman from Morocco had come to the village, he and his horse, and he had amazing children's shoes—unbelievably beautiful, elegant, and inexpensive shoes—which he was hoping to sell in advance of the upcoming holiday. No, I didn't stop playing to run off with the other children toward the Moroccan, who had set up shop at the square across from the mukhtar's guest house in order to display the beautiful children's shoes he was offering.

It may have been despair, or despondency, that gave rise to my response. Or maybe it was simply a matter of my being utterly helpless in the face of the situation, or perhaps it all came back to my indifference and apathy, which in turn sometimes evolved from my despondency and helplessness and despair.... The result was that I didn't run. And why should I? What good would my running there have done? What had changed? I was well aware that my barefoot condition couldn't be traced to any absence of shoe salesmen in the village. In fact, more than one store sold shoes, and one of the villagers even made them and would, with great pleasure, offer a pair to anyone willing to part with his pound and a half, or two. How many times had I passed the fine-looking shoes stacked on the shelves in the stores or set out in a row on their thrones in the small storefront window of Hamza's shop, where there were shoes whose colors ranged from the deep-red of twilight to a black that glimmered like starlings' wings to a dark chocolate brown—and also shoes whose two brilliant, marvelous tones enthralled the eye and truly enchanted the mind!

No, shoes of assorted colors and numerous kinds were plentiful enough in the village. They were, as they say, at hand. The problem, as far as I was concerned, was that they would never be *at foot.* In fact, I believed that the shoes would never really be within rocket range of my feet. My problem, which had neither solution nor resolution, and in the face of which I was helpless, lay in the principle of "forbidden fruits" or the law of "cash and carry," which governed one's dealing with shoes in general, whether it came to the stores in the village or to the Moroccan's saddlebags. It made little difference whether the merchant was from North Africa or the East or a nearby village, or even, should God so will it, from China. Why should I run? Why should I race toward what would inevitably lead to nothing more than a renewal of my bitterness? Did it matter that it would not be a local bitterness, but a fresh, imported, exotic one from the distant land of our brothers in the Maghreb?

I didn't run. I kept on playing my hopscotch, or looking for another scarab in another pile of dirt. For the Moroccan, as I recall the incident now quite well, woke in me at first no special interest or any unusual concern.

Moreover, for almost a year before the Moroccan's arrival, I had started to grow tired of dreaming in front of the shoe-store window. I would stand there looking, but without prolonging my gaze or lingering. A short stop, a glance or two, and then I would turn my back on the shoes and the grief and the heartache they brought on. I even started to ignore the price tags, and would read neither yesterday's crossed-out figures nor today's reduced prices. A short stop, a shorter look, and I'd be on my way, either to play with my friends, or—if it was threshing season—to go to the threshing floor that belonged to one of our relatives. I'd take a short, wild ride on the threshing-board pulled by his wonderful chestnut horse, or get off and go down to the fields to trap small birds and partridges with a snare I had made with my own two hands from old wires and the ribs of discarded umbrellas.

If it was winter and rainy, I would take advantage of the breaks between showers, roll up my pants to the knee, and plunge my feet into the water of one of the canals until they exhausted the depths of the channel and reached bottom. I would balance the timing of the movements of my upper body and legs with the movements of my arms, open in the air like the wings of a bird, and start to walk with the current in the canal, which sometimes curved around a bend and sometimes went straight, sweeping along with it rainwater from the neighborhood streets and roofs and alleys on its way to the vegetable gardens and the village fields.... I'd walk, stand, then walk in the water which usually covered my calf muscle, feeling against my bare legs and the flesh of my feet and the nerve-ends of my toes small pieces of metal, for the most part little coins with holes at their center, coins that had been lost by their owners and swept away by the water, or marbles, bullet casings, and old ladies' copper rings which had been thrown away by grandsons, and small keys, and sometimes bigger keys, in addition to crooked old nails, bent like the words of liars.

Sometimes I would find pieces of colored Roman glass, three or four amazing crystal beads which the rain had kicked up and released from the prison where they had been hidden only a short while ago, the currents of water having pushed them along in the flow, so that as they wound around and floated along, as they were thrown up and down and swept away, in front and then behind the current, they seemed to be dancing, rejoicing in their newfound freedom from their ancient Roman jail.

But my happiness was indescribable the day I stumbled across an old top, took off what was stuck to it, dried out its wood, and painted it with blue ink, until it looked brand new.

It's entirely possible that the joy I took in exploring, the pleasures of hunting and running around and playing, were experienced by none of the boys in the neighborhood in the same way that I experienced them, as most of them had shoes, something which denied them the delights of descending barefoot into the canal and feeling for things with their toes, then scooping them up skillfully from the water, and running back with them to the house, like a hero returning home with a prize—this, apart from my being almost absolutely convinced of the utter futility of my hope of ever owning a pair of shoes, now or at any time in the near future. Maybe all this was meant to keep me from having any sudden, jarring thoughts about shoes, or to keep my thoughts of them far from one another, to make sure they didn't act up, and to prevent any outbursts of longing. Sometimes, for a while or longer, all did in fact seem quiet—until, over the course of a year, I began to notice my tendency to reduce the amount of time I spent standing in front of the shoe-store window, and to shorten my stares at the shoes. I started making unconscious efforts as well to exclude the shoes from the field of my attention, to push them back into the furthest reaches of my mind.

(7)

What I wasn't prepared for, by God, what I was not prepared for came to pass when the sun was a dark-red jinn's eye gliding toward the horizon, rushing, gazing down as it neared the moment of its plunge behind the western hills. The cloven hooves of livestock, and the uncloven hooves of the other animals, and the feet of the farmers and shepherds returning from the pastures and fields raised up dust between the late-afternoon and twilight, and gray, burnt-looking clouds grew gloomy, hovering over the entrance to the village like clouds of smoke over the tents of kidnappers and gypsy thieves of pots and pans, shoes and lambs. It was just at this time that one of the neighborhood boys, Salim Amun, came and said something that made me throw down what was in my hand and ask him with a sigh of disbelief:

"Are you saying shoes for twenty piasters?"

Salim Amun answered, and I felt the sincerity of his words and the look in his eyes, the purest trust flowing through his lips:

"Yes, the Moroccan's shoes are only twenty piasters. It's incredible. If you don't believe me, go and see for yourself."

I rushed off, leaping higher than I'd ever imagined I could leap.... And so I arrived at the mukhtar's square.

After two additional surprising leaps, which startled the sorrel horse tied by its halter to a wooden peg driven into the ground some four or five meters from its owner, I found myself standing over the shoes, stroking them in my mind as I turned them over and over in my imagination. My concentration wasn't at all disturbed by the horse, which reared up on its back legs, raising its forelegs over its head, as it sent out the whinny of a strange, frightened animal. I paid no heed to the wearied voice of the man and the dried-up words he directed at his horse in order to calm it down. I didn't even look at the man's face, or notice his features. It was the shoes alone that occupied me. The shoes alone. Or what remained of the shoes that had been on display, spread out in a row on the flattened saddlebags on the ground before the squatting Moroccan, who was skinny and had a thick, black beard. The man would have held no interest for me at all, if it weren't for the fact that he was selling beautiful children's shoes for twenty piasters a pair. Only twenty piasters. No, the shoes themselves were what occupied me and made me oblivious to everything else in the square.

When I asked the man if what Salim Amun had said was true, he assured me, in his Moroccan dialect:

"That's correct, a pair for twenty francs."

"You mean, *a pair of shoes* for *twenty piasters?*" I asked the man, and he answered:

"That's right, twenty piasters. We say francs. Yes, a pair of shoes for twenty piasters."

(8)

I don't know how I got home: I ran with such speed and power that my feet barely touched the ground. The clouds of dust, burnt by the summer heat, were still riding over one another and lengthening continuously, as the caravans and herds advanced in the direction of the minaret and the upper part of the village, penetrating and crawling slowly toward the eastern olive groves. My mother was alone in the courtyard, and father joined us when he heard me burst into tears and say:

"Shoes for twenty a pair. Hurry before they're gone. Hurry, only twenty piasters a pair."

My mother said, sadly, "God help you, my child." I interrupted her with my pleading, but my father backed her up with his silence, completing her expression without having to utter a word. I cried out—for I, more than anyone, knew just what that help would be, and my cry was mixed with my bitter weeping and my weeping bled into my beseeching scream:

"Only twenty piasters, hurry, before they're gone, by God, or I'll throw myself into the well. Just twenty piasters."

And, suddenly ... a new page was turned. Mother drew near to Father and I heard her tell him: "... from Abu Abbas, and Um Kassam ... and I have eight." My father left for Abu Abbas's store, and my mother called out to Um Kassam, our neighbor, from whom we were separated by a waist-high wall of piled-up stones.

(9)

I flew on enchanted wings! Where are you, O my Moroccan?! I flew toward the thin old man with the black beard and the saddlebags laid out beneath the pairs of shoes which awaited me.... I was flying, and my mind began to fathom the secrets of flight, or at least the flight of children, and I grasped my twenty piasters tightly in my hand, being careful lest they slip out between my fingers. My feet lapped up the distance, and I soared.

The sun had set, and the dust had settled on the rocks of the foothills and the oak branches. The mukhtar's square was now utterly silent and still. There was no movement within it, not a sound, not a breeze, and this time the horse wasn't startled by my arrival. I observed that the Moroccan demonstrated no particular anticipation of this new buyer who might bring him an additional sale. He paid no attention to my appearance, and didn't seem to notice me standing there suddenly before him. In his right hand the man was holding two brown shoes. He was in the process of putting them into one of the saddlebags, which he grasped with his left hand. I spoke up, my breathing still heavy from the race to the square:

"Take the twenty piasters and give me the shoes!"

"There aren't any left."

And with some effort, I understood that he was telling me that nothing remained for me now, and I said to him, gesturing toward his right hand:

"That pair! Sell them to me. Here's the money."

And the man said to me, his words full of warm regret:

"But sir, these are no good. They're both for the right foot. They're useless."

"What do you mean, useless? Give them to me and take the twenty."

The man put the two brown shoes on the ground, and pointed to the toe of one of the two shoes, and then moved the gesture to the toe of the other. With a voice like thin copper wire, a voice that contained, it seemed to me, equal parts of my father's grief and my mother's sadness, and more than a few figures of speech which I did not understand, he started to explain the problem to me. From the movement of his lips and his gestures, and from his sorrowful tone, I understood what I could no longer avoid understanding: I understood that the two shoes were each for the right foot, and that no other shoes remained. I had come too late.

I gave no thought to the disadvantages of having two right shoes, or, for that matter, to the advantage of two lefts, and I didn't enter into any complicated calculations. I neither thought nor hesitated, but said to the man straight away:

"Right, right ... so what? Sell me the two shoes and I'll take care of the rest."

"But two right shoes aren't good for you. You can't walk with them."

"So what! What difference does it make whether they're right or left? It's none of your business. Sell them to me and it's a deal—that's that."

"They're both rights."

"So what! Sell them to me and don't worry about it."

After several rounds of this back and forth—the man saying "two rights are useless" and me repeating "so what," we ended up at the two takes: he took the twenty piasters and went off to the mukhtar's guest house, and I took the two right shoes and set off running for home!

The weather was stifling, the air unforgiving, the voices of the people, farm animals, and dogs were still, and I–I simply couldn't believe that I'd actually gotten my shoes!   As I approached the house, I imagined that the best way to conceal the two right shoes from the eyes of my father and mother was to put them on outside, and then, somehow, they would shift from the realm of being two singles into the realm of being a pair.... And so, with my new pair of shoes I'd enter the courtyard. After I'd taken a few steps, I'd come into our room where my parents couldn't help but see me, and, with the new brown shoes on my feet, I'd parade before them, like the rest of God's creatures, and hear them say: "Congratulations! God bless you." And I would respond: "May you be blessed ..." And they would notice nothing unusual.

That's how I pictured it.

Counting on this scenario, I stood at the entrance to the courtyard and put the shoes on the ground, then stepped into them. I raised my right foot high and put it down to take a firm step on the stone threshold of the courtyard, and then it was my left foot's turn.... I raised it up and sent it out to complete my first step toward the entrance, and, I don't know how, I stumbled and somehow fell to the ground.

I rose right away, my heart pounding wildly, and I tried to take another step. The right foot went well, and I put it where I wanted. The left, however, filled me with terror—and before executing the step this time, I cautiously approached the hard, level ground before me, which was empty of all that might trip one up. I moved my foot wisely, and raised it slowly and deliberately, and lowered it with great care, but, nevertheless, when my foot felt the ground and sensed I was standing securely on it and completing the line ... again it slipped and I stumbled. This fall was worse than the first. I landed on a harder spot, and the sound I produced brought my parents out of the house bareheaded and alarmed. They saw me stretched out flat, my forehead touching the ground.

My father rushed to lift me up, and my mother cried out anxiously:

"What happened to you, my dear? What happened? God protect you ... What happened?"

I told her, and the taste in my mouth wasn't far from that of salty earth:

"It's nothing, nothing, it's over. Nothing happened."

"What do you mean nothing?" said my father, taking hold of my hand.... And before I could think of trying to walk again, my father lowered his gaze from the small spot of warm blood on my lower lip to my new brown shoes:

"Khalid!" My father said sternly. "Take off those shoes!"

Trembling, I said:

"But, Papa ... why should I take them off?"

"They're both for the right foot. Take them off!"

"So what? What difference does it make?!"

"Take them off! Don't make me get angry at you!"

My father started to list the reasons for me, explaining how it wasn't possible to walk with shoes like these. My mother supported him:

"The man tricked you, my dear. Go and return them."

"Why should I return them?!"

"They're two rights."

"So what?"

And my father bellowed:

"Take them off!"

I starting sobbing, removing my new brown shoes, and I sobbed on my way back to the mukhtar's square, and I sobbed telling my story to the Moroccan with the thin build and the black beard, who gave me back the twenty piasters with what seemed an apology:

"I told you they weren't good for anything."

(11)

The following morning, while I wasn't really sleeping and yet not entirely awake, my face was still buried in the feathers of my pillow, wet with the acid mix of sweat and tears. My head pounding continuously with the rhythm of my rapid, disturbed pulse, hot with its hammering, I heard the voice of my mother—like the voice heard in a dream, brushing up against the outer shell of my consciousness but not quite settling into memory. It came to me from our side of the waist-high wall of piled-up stones. Mother was talking to our good neighbor, Um Kassam, returning the five piasters she had borrowed from her the day before, and thanking her.

"Bless you for your kindness, Um Kassam. We didn't need them, neighbor. God bless you a thousand times over. May God let us repay you for your favor. By God, Um Kassam, Khalid's eyes barely closed last night. He was hot as fire all night long, my sweet child ... every few minutes he'd start up with a fright and scream: 'So what?!' He'd seem to sleep for two minutes, and then he'd start up and cry out again: 'So what?! So what?! So what?!'"

*Taha Muhammad Ali was born in 1931 in the
Galilee village of Saffuriya. During the Arab–
Israeli war of 1948, he fled to Lebanon, together
with most of the inhabitants of his village. A year
later he slipped back across the border with his
family and settled in Nazareth, where he has lived
ever since. His books of poetry in Arabic include*
Fourth Qasida, Fooling the Killers, *and* Fire in
the Convent Graveyard.